Freezer Jams & Refrigerator Pickles

Easy Ways to Preserve Your Harvest

Things You'll Need:

- ✦ Measuring cups
- ✦ Wide-mouth funnel
- ✦ Ladle
- ✦ Wooden spoons
- ✦ Sturdy, non-reactive saucepans and bowls (such as glass, plastic or stainless steel; avoid aluminum, copper or cast iron)
- ✦ Storage containers with tight-fitting lids (food- and freezer-safe)

   a. For jams, jellies and chutneys, use small containers (up to 1 cup) so they set up well.

   b. For most pickles, choose larger, wide-mouth containers (pint, quart or larger) for easier packing and serving.

   c. Wash containers in hot soapy water and rinse well, or run them through the wash and rinse cycle in an automatic dishwasher. (If filling the containers with hot ingredients, keep containers and lids warm.)

Printed in the United States of America
by G&R Publishing Co.

Distributed By:

507 Industrial Street
Waverly, IA 50677

ISBN-13: 978-1-56383-410-3
ISBN-10: 1-56383-410-3
Item #7097

Freezer Fresh
& Refrigerator Ready

Preserving your garden produce in the refrigerator or freezer is quick and easy – and requires minimal equipment. But because the jams, jellies and pickled products in this book will not be processed in a hot water bath, they are not shelf stable and cannot be stored at room temperature. Most can be stored in the freezer for up to one year or in the refrigerator for several weeks or months. Once opened, use within a few weeks. (Be sure to label containers with the product name and date.)

Choose the freshest produce, without bruises, mold or insect damage. Fruits and vegetables should be ripe and somewhat firm; avoid underripe or overripe produce.

Use food-safe, freezer-safe glass or rigid plastic containers with tight-fitting lids. Zippered plastic freezer bags may be a good choice for some frozen items, and large batches of refrigerator pickles may be stored in plastic ice cream pails. Proper techniques and containers will help you enjoy fresh ripe produce long past their season!

In a Jam: Things to Know

+ Pectin helps jam and jelly form a gel and set up. It can be purchased in powdered or liquid form. Pay attention to the labels and buy the type needed for each recipe. Some are designed for "no or low sugar" recipes and others are "instant", made especially for no-cook freezer jams.

+ Sugar is important: it preserves, sweetens and helps pectin work. Don't use artificial sweeteners unless specified in recipe.

+ Uncooked fruit mixtures maintain the brightest color and fresh-picked taste. The set may be softer than cooked jams.

+ Some fruits will be cooked for a short time to break down the pulp and release flavors.

+ Always let jams and jellies set up or gel before placing containers in the freezer or refrigerator.

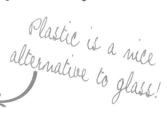

Plastic is a nice alternative to glass!

Jam Preps: 3 Ms

Mash: Crush ripe berries or other fruits with a potato masher or rigid pastry blender. If using a food processor, just pulse until finely chopped; do not puree unless directed to do so. Bits of fruit should remain in jams and marmalades.

Measure: Exact measurements are important for good results. Use a large liquid measuring cup to measure crushed fruit. Use dry measuring cups for sugar and level off with a straight edge.

Mix: Stir mixtures well so sugar dissolves and pectin is evenly dispersed before filling small containers.

In a Pickle: Things to Know

+ Vinegar, salt and/or sugar add flavor and preserve the vegetables being pickled.

+ Pickles are packed in liquid, like a salty brine or sweet syrup; vinegar and seasonings add unique flavors, which get stronger over time.

+ "Pickling spice" mixtures may be purchased in the spice aisle or you can make your own combinations.

+ Distilled white vinegar (5% acidity) works well, but apple cider vinegar or others can be used for a slightly different flavor and color.

+ Use pickling or non-iodized salt for clear brines. Never use rock salt.

+ Soft or distilled water is best for pickling; avoid hard water containing lime or other minerals.

+ Sugar adds crunch to pickles, and thick slices will stay crisp longer than thin ones.

Make sure your jars are freezer-safe!

4

Pickle Preps: 3 Ss

<u>Slice:</u> Cut vegetables or fruits into uniform pieces such as disks, spears, sticks or chunks. Do not peel cucumbers.

<u>Stuff:</u> Fit as much produce into the containers as possible before adding the brine or syrup, unless directed otherwise.

<u>Soak:</u> Mix the brine or syrup according to directions for good flavor, texture and long-lasting freshness. Pour it over the produce to soak.

Helpful Notes:

+ For a proper set, do not double or halve jam recipes.

+ Use fruits at room temperature to help sugar dissolve.

+ Do not overfill containers. Leave about ½" space ("headspace") at the top to allow for expansion during freezing.

+ To ensure the correct proportion of preservative ingredients, follow pickle recipes as written.

+ If pickles float on top of the brine or syrup, place a wad of waxed paper or heavy plate under the lid to keep the food submerged in the liquid.

+ Before tasting, let pickles stand in the refrigerator at least 24 hours to absorb seasonings – a week is even better.

+ Thaw frozen jam overnight in the refrigerator before using. Once opened, use within 3 weeks.

+ If you notice any off-color, odor, flavor or evidence of mold or other spoilage, discard product.

Jelly Jars come in all shapes and sizes!

MAKES
6 CUPS

Peach Melba Jam

- ✦ 1½ PTS. FRESH RASPBERRIES *
- ✦ 1 TO 2 RIPE PEACHES
- ✦ 1 TSP. ASCORBIC-CITRIC POWDER
  (SUCH AS FRUIT-FRESH)
- ✦ 4½ C. SUGAR
- ✦ 2 T. FINELY CHOPPED FRESH MINT, OPTIONAL
- ✦ 3 T. LEMON JUICE
- ✦ 1 (3 OZ.) POUCH LIQUID PECTIN

DIRECTIONS

In a large shallow bowl, crush raspberries; set aside. Peel**, pit and finely chop peaches. Measure out 1 cup chopped peaches into a large bowl. Sprinkle peaches with ascorbic-citric powder and stir to coat. Measure out 1½ cups crushed berries and add to peaches in bowl. Add sugar to fruit mixture and mix well. If desired, stir in mint. Let stand for 10 minutes; stir occasionally.

In a small bowl, mix lemon juice and pectin. Add to fruit mixture and stir well for 3 to 5 minutes, until sugar is dissolved. Ladle into small clean containers, leaving ½" headspace. Cover tightly and let stand at room temperature for 24 hours to set. Store containers in the refrigerator (for up to 3 weeks) or freezer (for up to 1 year).

* YOU MAY SUBSTITUTE 3 CUPS FROZEN RASPBERRIES, PARTIALLY THAWED, FOR THE FRESH BERRIES.

** TO PEEL PEACHES EASILY, PLACE WHOLE FRUIT IN BOILING WATER FOR 30 SECONDS. REMOVE AND PLUNGE INTO ICE WATER. PEEL OFF SKIN WITH A PARING KNIFE.

MAKES
1 QUART

One-Day Bread & Butter Pickles

- ✦ 2 MEDIUM CUCUMBERS
- ✦ ½ ONION
- ✦ ¾ C. DISTILLED WHITE VINEGAR
- ✦ ¾ C. SUGAR
- ✦ ¼ TSP. GROUND TURMERIC
- ✦ ¼ TSP. MUSTARD SEED
- ✦ ¼ TSP. CELERY SEED
- ✦ 4 TSP. PICKLING SALT

DIRECTIONS

Wash and thinly slice cucumbers (⅛" to ¼"). Thinly slice onion and separate into rings. In a spouted bowl, combine vinegar, sugar, turmeric, mustard seed, celery seed and salt; stir until well blended. Pour mixture into a quart-size glass jar with tight-fitting lid. Add cucumbers and onion to jar in alternating layers. Cover tightly and turn jar upside down on the counter for 2 hours. Turn jar right side up and place in refrigerator. Let stand for at least 24 hours before eating. Pickles may be stored in the refrigerator for up to 3 months.

NOTE: TO MAKE ONE GALLON OF PICKLES, INCREASE THE RECIPE BY FOUR AND PLACE ALL INGREDIENTS IN A ONE-GALLON GLASS JAR.

Makes
7 cups

Peach Jam

- ✦ 2 C. MASHED RIPE PEACHES *
- ✦ 2 TSP. ASCORBIC-CITRIC POWDER
  (SUCH AS FRUIT-FRESH)
- ✦ 4 C. SUGAR
- ✦ 2 T. LEMON JUICE
- ✦ ¼ TSP. GROUND CINNAMON
- ✦ 1 (3 OZ.) POUCH LIQUID FRUIT PECTIN

DIRECTIONS

In a large microwave-safe bowl, stir together peaches and ascorbic-citric powder. Add sugar, lemon juice and cinnamon; mix until well blended. Microwave uncovered on high power for 5 minutes; remove and stir well. Return to microwave and cook on high for 5 to 6 minutes longer or until mixture reaches a full rolling boil for 1 minute. With hot pads, remove bowl and stir in pectin. Skim off foam with a spoon.

Ladle hot jam into clean warm containers, leaving ½" headspace. Cover tightly and cool to room temperature. Let stand for up to 24 hours or until set. Store containers in the refrigerator (for up to 3 weeks) or freezer (for up to 1 year).

* TO PEEL PEACHES EASILY, PLACE WHOLE FRUIT IN BOILING WATER FOR 30 SECONDS. REMOVE AND PLUNGE INTO ICE WATER. PEEL OFF SKIN WITH A PARING KNIFE. THEN CHOP AND MASH.

MAKES
1 PINT

PICKLED BEANS

- ✦ 5 OZ. FRESH GREEN AND/OR WAX BEANS
- ✦ 1 SPRIG FRESH DILL
- ✦ ½ C. DISTILLED WATER
- ✦ 1 C. APPLE CIDER VINEGAR
- ✦ ¼ TSP. MINCED GARLIC
- ✦ 1 TSP. PICKLING SPICE
- ✦ 1 T. SUGAR
- ✦ 1 TSP. PICKLING SALT

DIRECTIONS

Wash beans and snip off both ends. Place dill in a pint jar. Fill jar with beans, standing them up on end and packing jar full. Trim beans as needed; set aside.

In a small saucepan over high heat, combine water, vinegar, garlic, pickling spice, sugar and salt. Bring to a boil, stirring occasionally. Pour hot liquid over beans in jar. Cover tightly and let stand at room temperature until cool. Refrigerate for 24 hours before eating. Store in the refrigerator for up to 1 month.

NOTE: TO ADD HEAT, ADD A SPLIT JALAPEÑO PEPPER TO THE JAR.

SERVING SUGGESTIONS: SERVE IN SALADS, AS AN ACCOMPANIMENT TO MEAT AND POULTRY DISHES OR IN ADDITION TO CELERY STALKS IN A BLOODY MARY DRINK.

MAKES
4½ CUPS

BLACKBERRY-
RASPBERRY JAM

- ✦ 2 TO 3 PTS. FRESH BLACKBERRIES
- ✦ 1½ TO 2 PTS. FRESH RASPBERRIES
- ✦ 1¾ C. UNSWEETENED CRANBERRY-BLEND
  JUICE OR APPLE JUICE
- ✦ 3 T. POWDERED FRUIT PECTIN
  (FOR LESS OR NO SUGAR NEEDED RECIPES)
- ✦ 2½ TO 3 C. SUGAR *

DIRECTIONS

In a large shallow bowl, crush blackberries well. Measure out 2 cups crushed berries and transfer to another bowl. In the same way, crush the raspberries. Measure out 1 cup crushed berries and add to crushed blackberries; stir to blend and set aside.

In a large saucepan over medium-high heat, mix cranberry-blend juice and pectin powder, stirring to dissolve. Bring to a full rolling boil and boil for 1 minute, stirring constantly. Remove from heat and immediately add crushed berries. Stir fruit and hot pectin mixture for 1 minute. Add sugar and stir for 3 minutes more or until sugar is dissolved.

Ladle jam into small clean containers, leaving ½" headspace. Let cool. Cover tightly and let stand at room temperature for 2 to 3 hours to set up. Store containers in the refrigerator (for up to 3 weeks) or freezer (for up to 1 year).

* You MAY SUBSTITUTE EITHER ¾ TO 1 CUP HONEY OR 1½ CUPS SPLENDA GRANULATED NO CALORIE SWEETENER FOR THE SUGAR IN THIS RECIPE.

MAKES
8 CUPS

FREEZER COLE SLAW

- ✦ 1 MEDIUM HEAD GREEN CABBAGE
- ✦ 1 MEDIUM CARROT
- ✦ 1 TSP. PICKLING SALT
- ✦ 1 C. DISTILLED WHITE VINEGAR
- ✦ 2 C. SUGAR
- ✦ 1 TSP. CELERY SEED
- ✦ 1 TSP. MUSTARD SEED

DIRECTIONS

Wash cabbage and cut into quarters. Thinly slice or shred and place in a large bowl. Peel and shred carrot; add to bowl. Sprinkle vegetables with salt and stir well to coat. Let stand for 1 to 2 hours to draw out moisture.

In a small bowl, combine vinegar, sugar, celery seed and mustard seed; mix well. Lightly rinse and drain cabbage mixture; press out all excess liquid. In a large bowl, combine cabbage mixture and vinegar mixture; stir to coat thoroughly. Put mixture into a zippered one-gallon plastic freezer bag, pressing out all air. Freeze for up to 3 months. Thaw cabbage about 8 hours in the refrigerator and serve chilled. Use within 2 days after thawing.

NOTE: YOU MAY ADD SHREDDED ONION AND/OR GREEN BELL PEPPER TO MIXTURE BEFORE THE SALTING PROCESS.

MAKES
2 CUPS

LEMON CURD

- ✦ 6 LARGE EGG YOLKS
- ✦ ¾ C. SUGAR
- ✦ GRATED ZEST OF 1 LARGE LEMON
- ✦ 1 C. FRESH LEMON JUICE (5 MEDIUM LEMONS)
- ✦ ½ C. COLD BUTTER, CUT INTO 8 PIECES

Directions

Set a sieve over a heavy saucepan and press egg yolks through it to remove all egg whites; discard whites. Add sugar, lemon zest and lemon juice to saucepan; whisk until just combined. Place pan over medium heat and cook, stirring constantly, for 15 to 20 minutes or until mixture coats the back of a wooden spoon. Remove from heat. Add butter, one piece at a time, and stir after each addition so mixture is smooth.

Ladle lemon curd into small clean containers, leaving ½" headspace. Let stand at room temperature about 1 hour to set. Cover tightly and store containers in the refrigerator (for up to 3 weeks) or freezer (for up to 3 months).

NOTE: TRY MAKING ORANGE CURD BY USING ORANGE ZEST AND ORANGE JUICE IN PLACE OF LEMON ZEST AND JUICE.

SERVING SUGGESTIONS: USE LEMON CURD TO MAKE PIES AND TARTS. SERVE IT ON CAKE (POUND, SPONGE OR ANGEL FOOD), WAFFLES, PANCAKES, TOAST, BISCUITS OR HOT SCONES.

MAKES
1 QUART

GARDEN PICKLES

+ 4 C. SLICED CUCUMBERS
+ ½ C. THINLY SLICED ONION
+ ½ C. CUBED CELERY
+ ½ GREEN BELL PEPPER, CUT INTO STRIPS
+ ½ RED BELL PEPPER, CUT INTO STRIPS
+ 2¼ TSP. PICKLING SALT
+ ½ C. DISTILLED WHITE VINEGAR
+ 1 C. SUGAR
+ ½ TSP. CELERY SEED
+ ½ TSP. MUSTARD SEED

DIRECTIONS

In a large bowl, combine cucumbers, onion, celery and
both bell peppers. Sprinkle with salt and toss gently.
Let stand 1 to 2 hours. Meanwhile, in a microwave-safe
bowl, combine vinegar, sugar, celery seed and mustard
seed. Microwave on high power for 2 minutes to boil;
stir to dissolve sugar. Let cool.

Drain vegetables but do not rinse. Pour cool vinegar
mixture over vegetables and toss well. Ladle mixture
into a clean 1-quart jar with tight-fitting lid. Add a wad
of waxed paper to submerge vegetables in liquid as
needed. Cover tightly and refrigerate for up to 6 weeks.

CUCUMBER TIP: AVOID WAX-COATED CUCUMBERS FROM
GROCERY STORES BECAUSE THE PICKLING SOLUTION
HAS A HARD TIME PENETRATING THE COATING.

CITRUS MARMALADE

- 2 TO 3 ORANGES
- 1 LEMON
- 4 C. SUGAR *
- ¼ C. LEMON JUICE
- 1 (3 OZ.) POUCH LIQUID FRUIT PECTIN

DIRECTIONS

Using a zester or vegetable peeler, slice very thin strips of orange rind to get ¼ cup; slice very thin strips of lemon rind to get 2 tablespoons. Combine orange and lemon rinds in a small saucepan; cover with cold water and bring to a boil over high heat. Reduce heat, cover and boil gently for 15 minutes or until tender; drain.

Meanwhile, peel oranges and dice the flesh; place 1½ cups orange pieces in a large bowl. Slice lemon, cut off remaining rind and dice the flesh; place ¼ cup lemon pieces in bowl with oranges. Add sugar and cooked rind; stir well. Let stand for 10 minutes, stirring occasionally.

Add lemon juice and pectin; stir constantly for 5 minutes or until sugar is mostly dissolved. Ladle marmalade into small clean containers, leaving ½" headspace. Cover tightly and let stand at room temperature to set, up to 24 hours. Store containers in the refrigerator (for up to 3 weeks) or freezer (for up to 1 year).

* TO HELP SUGAR DISSOLVE, WARM SUGAR IN A SHALLOW PAN IN A 250° OVEN FOR 15 MINUTES BEFORE COMBINING WITH FRUIT.

MAKES
4 CUPS

PICKLED BEETS

- ✦ 5 MEDIUM FRESH BEETS
- ✦ ½ C. BROWN SUGAR
- ✦ ¾ C. DISTILLED WHITE
  VINEGAR
- ✦ 2 CINNAMON STICKS
- ✦ 4 WHOLE CLOVES

- ✦ 4 WHOLE ALLSPICE
- ✦ 4 TO 6 PEPPERCORNS
- ✦ ½ TSP. GROUND NUTMEG
- ✦ 1½ T. PREPARED
  HORSERADISH

Directions

Scrub beets and cut off stems, leaving about 1". Leave roots on. Put beets in a large pot and cover with water. Place over medium-high heat and bring to a boil. Cover and simmer for 20 to 30 minutes or until tender. Drain; plunge into cold water and let stand until cool. Trim off roots and slip off skins, using a spoon to avoid cutting flesh. Thinly slice or cut into ¾" cubes. Pack into clean containers.

In a medium saucepan over medium-high heat, combine ¾ cup water, brown sugar, vinegar, cinnamon sticks, cloves, allspice, peppercorns and nutmeg. Stir and bring to a boil. Reduce heat and simmer uncovered for 10 minutes. Remove from heat and whisk in horseradish. Strain liquid into a spouted measuring cup. Pour liquid over beets in containers until covered. Cover containers tightly and refrigerate for 2 to 3 days before serving. Store in the refrigerator for up to 1 month.

SERVING SUGGESTIONS: SERVE AS AN ACCOMPANIMENT TO MEATS, POULTRY OR CASSEROLES, OR ADD TO A RELISH TRAY.

MAKES
6 CUPS

BLUEBERRY-
PEACH JAM

- ✦ 4 C. FRESH RIPE BLUEBERRIES
- ✦ 2 LARGE RIPE PEACHES
- ✦ ¼ C. LEMON JUICE
- ✦ 5 C. SUGAR
- ✦ 1 (1.75 OZ.) PKG. POWDERED FRUIT PECTIN

DIRECTIONS

In a large shallow bowl, crush blueberries thoroughly. Measure out 2 cups crushed berries and transfer to a large bowl; set aside.

Peel*, pit and finely chop peaches. Measure out 1 cup chopped peaches and add to blueberries; mix well. Stir in lemon juice and then sugar until well blended. Let stand for 10 minutes, stirring several times.

Meanwhile, in a small saucepan, stir together ¾ cup water and pectin powder until dissolved. Bring to a boil over high heat, stirring constantly; boil and stir for 1 minute. Add hot pectin mixture to fruit mixture and stir for 3 minutes or until sugar is mostly dissolved.

Ladle jam into small warm containers immediately, leaving ½" headspace. Cover tightly and let stand at room temperature for 24 hours. Store containers in the refrigerator (for up to 3 weeks) or freezer (for up to 1 year).

* TO PEEL PEACHES EASILY, PLACE WHOLE FRUIT IN BOILING WATER FOR 30 SECONDS. REMOVE AND PLUNGE INTO ICE WATER. PEEL OFF SKIN WITH A PARING KNIFE.

MAKES
1 GALLON

A Pickle Pot

- 2 TO 3 MEDIUM CUCUMBERS
- 4 LARGE CARROTS
- 1 HEAD CAULIFLOWER
- 1 ONION
- ½ LB. GREEN TOMATOES
- ½ LB. FRESH GREEN OR WAX BEANS, HALVED
- 2 CLOVES GARLIC, PEELED AND LEFT WHOLE
- 1 T. DRIED DILL WEED
- 3 C. DISTILLED WHITE VINEGAR
- 3 C. SUGAR
- ⅓ C. PICKLING SALT

DIRECTIONS

Cut cucumbers into ¼" to ½" slices. Peel carrots and cut into 1" chunks. Trim cauliflower and separate into medium florets. Chop onion into large chunks. Cut tomatoes into quarters. Trim ends off beans and cut in half. In a medium saucepan of boiling water, blanch carrots for 2 minutes; drain and rinse carrots in cold water.

Layer all vegetables as desired in a one-gallon jar or ice cream pail, placing garlic in the middle and packing container tightly. Sprinkle with dill weed. In a large bowl, combine vinegar, sugar and salt; stir for 5 minutes until mostly dissolved. Pour liquid over vegetables. Cover container and refrigerate for 24 hours before eating. If vegetables float, press down with a wad of waxed paper or set a plate on top to keep vegetables submerged in liquid. Store in the refrigerator for up to 1 month.

NOTE: YOU MAY ADD MORE VEGETABLES TO THE PICKLE POT. MIX AND ADD ADDITIONAL BRINE TO COVER THEM AS NEEDED (1 CUP VINEGAR, 1 CUP SUGAR AND 1 TABLESPOON SALT).

MAKES
5 CUPS

STRAWBERRY- MANGO JAM

- ✦ 2½ TO 3 PTS. FRESH RIPE STRAWBERRIES
- ✦ 1 TO 2 RIPE MANGOS
- ✦ 1 LIME
- ✦ 1½ C. SUGAR *
- ✦ 1 (1.59 OZ.) POUCH POWDERED INSTANT FRUIT PECTIN (SCANT ¼ C.)

DIRECTIONS

Hull clean strawberries. In a large shallow bowl, thoroughly crush 1 cup berries at a time. Measure out 3 cups crushed berries and transfer to a large bowl; set aside. Peel and pit mango(s) and cut up flesh. Place mango pieces in a bowl and mash well. Measure out 1 cup mashed mango and add to strawberries. Grate zest from lime and add to fruit with 1 tablespoon lime juice. Stir well to blend.

In a medium bowl, stir together sugar and pectin powder until well mixed. Add to fruit mixture and stir for 3 minutes. Ladle jam into small clean jars, leaving ½" headspace. Cover tightly and let stand at room temperature for 1 hour or until thickened and set. Store containers in the refrigerator (for up to 3 weeks) or freezer (for up to 1 year).

* SPLENDA GRANULATED NO CALORIE SWEETENER MAY BE SUBSTITUTED FOR THE SUGAR IN THIS RECIPE. USE THE SAME QUANTITY. DO NOT USE OTHER ARTIFICIAL SWEETENERS.

MAKES
3 CUPS

SWEET & HOT PEARL ONIONS

- 2 (10 OZ.) PKGS. SMALL PEARL ONIONS (23/4 C.)
- 1 C. SUGAR
- 1 C. DISTILLED WHITE VINEGAR
- 1½ T. PACKAGED BREAD AND BUTTER PICKLE MIX (SUCH AS MRS. WAGES)
- ½ TSP. RED PEPPER FLAKES, OR TO TASTE

DIRECTIONS

In a large saucepan of boiling water, blanch onions to loosen skin, about 3 minutes. Drain; rinse in cold water. Slide skins off onions, trimming root end slightly as needed. Set onions aside and discard skins.

In a large saucepan over medium-high heat, combine sugar, vinegar, pickle mix and red pepper flakes. Bring mixture to a full rolling boil, stirring several times. Add onions and turn off heat. Cover and let stand for 5 minutes. Ladle hot onions and liquid into clean warm containers. Cover tightly and let stand at room temperature for 1 hour to cool. Transfer to the refrigerator to store for up to 3 months.

SERVING SUGGESTIONS: GARNISH COLD MEAT SANDWICHES OR ADD TO MEAT AND CHEESE PLATTERS. SERVE AS AN ACCOMPANIMENT TO ROAST BEEF OR GRILLED MEATS.

Makes
3 cups

Zippy Plum Chutney

- ✦ 7 to 8 red plums *
- ✦ ½ C. finely chopped red onion
- ✦ ½ C. sugar
- ✦ ½ C. golden raisins
- ✦ Juice of 1 large orange (⅓ C.)
- ✦ ⅓ C. apple cider vinegar
- ✦ 3 cloves garlic, minced
- ✦ 1 tsp. ground allspice
- ✦ 1 tsp. ground cumin
- ✦ 1 tsp. ground coriander
- ✦ 1 tsp. salt

DIRECTIONS

Pit and chop plums. Measure out 3½ cups chopped plums into a large saucepan. Add onion, sugar, raisins, orange juice, vinegar, garlic, allspice, cumin, coriander and salt; mix well. Place pan over medium-high heat and bring mixture to a boil. Reduce heat to medium-low, cover and simmer for 20 minutes. Uncover and cook for 20 to 30 minutes or until thickened to desired consistency, stirring occasionally.

Remove from heat and let cool for 20 minutes. Ladle chutney into small clean containers, leaving ½" headspace. When almost cool, cover tightly. Store containers in the refrigerator (for up to 3 weeks) or freezer (for up to 1 year).

* SOME RED PLUMS ARE RED INSIDE AND OTHERS ARE PALE. YOU MAY USE EITHER TYPE OR A COMBINATION OF THE TWO.

SERVING SUGGESTIONS: SERVE WITH GRILLED PORK, CHICKEN OR FISH, OR USE AS A CONDIMENT WITH PITAS OR HAM SANDWICHES.

MAKES
2½ CUPS

Pickled Hot Peppers

- ✦ 7 MEDIUM JALAPEÑO PEPPERS
- ✦ 4 SMALL HABANERO PEPPERS
- ✦ 2 C. DISTILLED WHITE VINEGAR
- ✦ 1 TSP. SUGAR
- ✦ 1 TSP. PICKLING SALT
- ✦ 1 T. BLACK PEPPERCORNS
- ✦ 1 T. MINCED GARLIC
- ✦ 1 T. MUSTARD SEED

DIRECTIONS

Slice jalapeño and habanero peppers into rings, removing
most of the white membrane and keeping only
¼ to ½ of the seeds; combine in a bowl and set aside.

In a large saucepan over medium-high heat, combine
vinegar, sugar, salt, peppercorns, garlic and mustard
seed. Bring mixture to a full boil. Add peppers; stir just
to coat and remove from heat to maintain crispness.
Ladle peppers into clean warm containers, covering
pepper rings with liquid. Cover tightly and let stand
at room temperature for 1 hour to cool. Transfer
to the refrigerator and let stand for at least 3 days
before eating. Pickled peppers may be stored in the
refrigerator for up to 3 weeks. Leftover peppers may
be frozen for longer storage.

SERVING SUGGESTIONS: SERVE AS A RELISH WITH
SANDWICHES OR CASSEROLES, ADD TO SOUPS OR
GARNISH MEXICAN ENTRÉES.

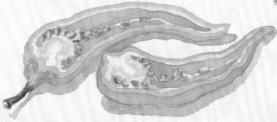

MAKES
6 CUPS

PUCKER-UP APRICOT PINEAPPLE JAM

- 1½ C. SUGAR
- 1 (1.59 OZ.) POUCH POWDERED INSTANT FRUIT PECTIN (SCANT ¼ C.)
- 11 TO 12 FRESH RIPE APRICOTS
- 1 (8 OZ.) CAN CRUSHED PINEAPPLE, UNDRAINED
- 1 T. LIME JUICE

DIRECTIONS

In a large bowl, stir together sugar and pectin powder until well blended; set aside.

Peel*, pit and finely chop apricots. Place in a large shallow bowl and thoroughly crush the fruit, one portion at a time. Transfer 3 cups crushed apricots to another bowl. Add pineapple and lime juice to apricots; stir to blend. Add fruit mixture to reserved sugar-pectin mixture and stir for 3 minutes.

Ladle jam into small clean containers, leaving ½" headspace. Cover tightly and let stand at room temperature for at least 30 minutes or up to 5 hours to set. Store containers in the refrigerator (for up to 3 weeks) or freezer (for up to 1 year).

* TO PEEL APRICOTS EASILY, PLACE WHOLE FRUIT IN BOILING WATER FOR 30 SECONDS. REMOVE AND PLUNGE INTO ICE WATER. PEEL OFF SKIN WITH A PARING KNIFE.

GRAPE JELLY

- ✦ 1½ LBS. RIPE CONCORD GRAPES
  (2 C. GRAPE JUICE *)
- ✦ 4 C. SUGAR
- ✦ 1 (3 OZ.) POUCH LIQUID FRUIT PECTIN

DIRECTIONS

Remove stems from grapes; place a layer of grapes in a large bowl and crush thoroughly. Add more grapes and crush, repeating until all are crushed.

In a large saucepan over medium-high heat, combine crushed grapes and ⅔ cup water. Bring to a boil and cover pan. Reduce heat to low and simmer for 15 minutes, stirring occasionally. Arrange three layers of damp cheesecloth or muslin in a large colander inside a large bowl. Pour hot fruit into cheesecloth and tie it closed at the top. Prop colander above the bowl until all the juice drips into bowl. Press gently to extract more juice, but avoid pressing out any pulp or jelly will become cloudy. Measure 2 cups juice into a large bowl. Add sugar and stir well for 3 minutes; let stand for 10 minutes, stirring occasionally.

In a small bowl, mix pectin and 2 tablespoons water. Add to juice mixture and stir for 3 minutes or until sugar is mostly dissolved. Ladle jelly into small clean containers, leaving ½" headspace. Cover and let stand for 24 hours until gel has formed. Store containers in the refrigerator (for up to 3 weeks) or freezer (for up to 1 year).

★ YOU MAY ALSO MAKE THIS JELLY FROM UNSWEETENED GRAPE JUICE (BOTTLED, CANNED OR FROZEN GRAPE JUICE CONCENTRATE MIXED WITH WATER).

MAKES
4 CUPS

RHUBARB JAM

- ✦ 7½ C. SLICED FRESH RHUBARB
  (ABOUT 2½ LBS.)
- ✦ 2 C. SUGAR
- ✦ 2 TSP. GRATED ORANGE ZEST
- ✦ ⅓ C. ORANGE JUICE CONCENTRATE OR FRESH
  ORANGE JUICE
- ✦ 2 TO 3 DROPS RED FOOD COLORING

DIRECTIONS

In a large saucepan over medium-high heat, combine rhubarb, sugar, orange zest, orange juice concentrate and ½ cup water. Bring mixture to a boil, stirring frequently. Reduce heat to medium-low and cook for 45 minutes, stirring occasionally, until thick.

Remove from heat and stir in food coloring. Ladle jam into small warm containers, leaving ½" headspace. Cover tightly and cool to room temperature. Let stand for up to 24 hours until set. Store containers in the refrigerator (for up to 3 weeks) or freezer (for up to 1 year).

NOTE: YOU MAY ALSO USE SLICED FROZEN RHUBARB AND COOK AS DIRECTED.

MAKES
6 CUPS

STRAWBERRY JAM

- ✦ 4 PTS. FRESH RIPE STRAWBERRIES
- ✦ 3 C. SUGAR
- ✦ 1 (1.75 OZ.) PKG. POWDERED FRUIT PECTIN
  (FOR LESS OR NO SUGAR NEEDED RECIPES)

DIRECTIONS

Hull clean strawberries. In a large shallow bowl, crush
1 cup strawberries at a time. Measure out 4 cups
crushed berries and transfer to a large bowl; set aside.

In a large saucepan, mix sugar and pectin powder until
well blended. Stir in 1 cup water. Bring mixture to a boil
over medium-high heat, stirring constantly; boil and stir
for 1 minute. Remove from heat. Quickly add crushed
berries to hot sugar-pectin mixture; stir for 1 minute or
until well mixed.

Ladle jam into small clean containers, leaving ½" headspace.
Cover and let stand at room temperature for 24 hours
until set. Store containers in the refrigerator (for up to
3 weeks) or freezer (for up to 1 year).

MAKES
4 CUPS

APPLE BUTTER

+ 1 C. SUGAR
+ ½ C. BROWN SUGAR
+ 5 T. POWDERED INSTANT FRUIT PECTIN
+ ½ TSP. GROUND CINNAMON
+ ½ TSP. GROUND APPLE PIE SPICE
+ 5 C. PEELED, CORED, COARSELY CHOPPED APPLES *
+ 1 T. LEMON JUICE

DIRECTIONS

In a large bowl, stir together sugar, brown sugar, pectin powder, cinnamon and apple pie spice until well blended; set aside. Place chopped apples and lemon juice in a food processor or blender; process until smooth. Add apple puree to sugar mixture and stir for 3 minutes to blend well.

Ladle apple mixture into small clean containers, leaving ½" headspace. Cover tightly and let stand at room temperature until thickened, about 30 minutes. Store containers in the refrigerator (for up to 3 weeks) or freezer (for up to 1 year).

* TRY GRANNY SMITH, MCINTOSH OR JONATHAN APPLES.

SERVING SUGGESTIONS: SERVE WITH COTTAGE CHEESE, OATMEAL, PORK CHOPS, HAM OR TURKEY, OR SPREAD THE APPLE BUTTER ON WARM MUFFINS, BISCUITS, ROLLS OR TOAST.

MAKES
½ GALLON

REFRIGERATED DILL SPEARS

+ ½ C. DISTILLED WHITE VINEGAR
+ ½ C. APPLE CIDER VINEGAR
+ ¼ C. PICKLING SALT
+ 3 TO 4 MEDIUM CUCUMBERS
+ 4 TO 5 SPRIGS FRESH DILL, DIVIDED
+ 1 T. PICKLING SPICE
+ 3 CLOVES GARLIC, HALVED

DIRECTIONS

In a large saucepan over medium-high heat, combine 5½ cups water, both vinegars and salt. Bring to a boil, stirring several times; boil for 3 minutes. Remove from heat and let cool.

Wash cucumbers and slice in half crosswise. Cut pieces in half lengthwise and then cut into spears (approximately 12 spears from each cucumber). Place half of dill sprigs in a clean plastic 5-quart ice cream pail. Add cucumber spears, pickling spice, garlic and remaining dill sprigs. Pour cool vinegar mixture over cucumbers. Set a plate on top and press down lightly to submerge cucumbers in liquid. Cover and let stand at room temperature for 24 hours, stirring once or twice, if desired. Place pail in the refrigerator to store pickles for up to 1 month.

NOTE: THIS BRINE CAN ALSO BE USED TO SOAK WHOLE BABY CUCUMBERS. RECIPE MAY BE DOUBLED TO FILL THE PAIL.

CHERRY RHUBARB JAM

- 3½ C. SLICED FRESH RHUBARB (ABOUT 1¼ LBS.)

- 2 C. SUGAR

- 1 C. CHERRY PIE FILLING, COARSELY CHOPPED

- 1 (3 OZ.) PKG. CHERRY GELATIN

DIRECTIONS

In a large saucepan over medium-high heat, combine
rhubarb and ⅔ cup water. Bring to a boil and cook until
tender, about 2 minutes. Stir in sugar and cook for
3 minutes more. Add pie filling and cook for 8 minutes,
stirring constantly. Remove from heat and add gelatin.
Stir several minutes until gelatin is dissolved.

Ladle jam into small warm containers. Cover tightly and
cool to room temperature. Let stand for up to 24 hours
until set. Store containers in the refrigerator (for up to
3 weeks) or freezer (for up to 1 year).

MAKES
1 QUART

Pickled Veggie Blend

- ✦ 2 SMALL ZUCCHINI
- ✦ 1 SMALL YELLOW SQUASH
- ✦ 2 MEDIUM CARROTS
- ✦ 1 MEDIUM SWEET RED BELL PEPPER
- ✦ 1 C. SUGAR
- ✦ 2 TSP. PICKLING SPICE
- ✦ ⅔ C. DISTILLED WHITE VINEGAR

Directions

Slice zucchini and squash into rounds, ½" thick. Peel carrots and slice into sticks, about 1½" long and ½" wide. Core and seed bell pepper; slice into sticks, about 1½" long and ½" wide. Pack zucchini into the bottom of a clean 1-quart container, with cut sides of outer slices facing out. Arrange carrots and peppers standing upright on top of zucchini. Layer squash rounds on top with cut sides of outer slices facing out. Set aside.

In a medium saucepan over medium heat, combine 1 cup water, sugar and pickling spice. Bring mixture to a boil; reduce heat and simmer uncovered, without stirring, for 5 minutes. Cool to room temperature. Stir in vinegar. Slowly pour liquid into container to cover vegetables. Top with a wad of waxed paper to keep vegetables submerged in liquid. Cover tightly and refrigerate for up to 3 weeks.

SERVING SUGGESTIONS: ADD TO A RELISH TRAY OR SERVE AS AN ACCOMPANIMENT WITH SANDWICHES, CASSEROLES OR MEAT DISHES.

STRAWBERRY CHUTNEY

- ¼ C. CHOPPED DRIED PINEAPPLE
- ¼ C. BROWN SUGAR
- ¼ C. LEMON JUICE
- ¼ C. DISTILLED WHITE VINEGAR
- 2 T. HONEY
- 2 C. SLICED FRESH STRAWBERRIES
- 1 TSP. RASPBERRY FLAVORING

DIRECTIONS

In a medium saucepan, combine pineapple, brown sugar, lemon juice, vinegar and honey. Stir to blend and place over medium-high heat. Bring mixture to a boil. Reduce heat to medium and cook for 15 minutes or until slightly thick. Stir in strawberries. Reduce heat to low and simmer uncovered for 10 minutes or until thick, stirring occasionally. Remove from heat; stir in raspberry flavoring.

Let stand at room temperature for 1 hour. Ladle into small clean containers, leaving ½" headspace. Cover tightly and store containers in the refrigerator (for up to 3 weeks) or freezer (for up to 1 year).

SERVING SUGGESTIONS: SPREAD ROUND BUTTER CRACKERS WITH CREAM CHEESE AND TOP WITH STRAWBERRY CHUTNEY TO SERVE AS AN APPETIZER, OR SERVE AS A CONDIMENT WITH A MEAT, CHEESE AND CRACKER PLATTER.

MAKES
3½ CUPS

PINEAPPLE-KIWI JAM

- ✦ 4 KIWIFRUIT
- ✦ 3 C. SUGAR
- ✦ 1 (8 OZ.) CAN CRUSHED PINEAPPLE, UNDRAINED
- ✦ ¼ C. LIME JUICE
- ✦ 1 (3 OZ.) POUCH LIQUID FRUIT PECTIN
- ✦ 3 DROPS GREEN FOOD COLORING, OPTIONAL

DIRECTIONS

Peel and thinly slice kiwifruit. In a large microwave-safe
bowl, combine kiwifruit, sugar, pineapple and lime juice;
stir well. Microwave uncovered on high power about
8 minutes, stirring every 2 minutes, until mixture comes
to a full rolling boil. With hot pads, remove bowl and
stir in pectin. If large pieces of fruit remain, break up
with potato masher to desired consistency. Stir in food
coloring, if desired.

Ladle jam into small warm containers, leaving ½" headspace;
let cool. Cover tightly and let stand at room temperature
overnight or until set, up to 24 hours. Store containers
in the refrigerator (for up to 3 weeks) or freezer (for
up to 1 year).

MAKES
4 CUPS

CORN RELISH

- 3 C. COOKED CORN KERNELS *
  (4 TO 5 MEDIUM EARS)
- 1¼ C. DICED BELL PEPPER
  (ANY COLOR)
- ½ C. FINELY CHOPPED ONION
- 1¼ C. DISTILLED
  WHITE VINEGAR
- ¾ C. SUGAR
- 1 TSP. CELERY SEED
- 1 TSP. MUSTARD SEED
- 1 TSP. PICKLING SALT
- ¼ TSP. RED
  PEPPER FLAKES
- 1 T. CORNSTARCH

DIRECTIONS

In a large bowl, combine corn, bell pepper and onion; set aside. In a large saucepan over medium-high heat, combine vinegar, sugar, celery seed, mustard seed, salt and red pepper flakes. Bring to a boil, stirring frequently. Add vegetables and return to a boil, stirring several times. Reduce heat to low and simmer uncovered for about 10 minutes. Spoon off any foam.

In a small bowl, mix cornstarch and 2 tablespoons water; pour into corn mixture and cook over medium heat for 3 to 5 minutes, stirring occasionally, until mixture starts to thicken. Ladle hot mixture into clean warm jars. Cover tightly and let stand at room temperature for 2 hours to cool. Transfer to the refrigerator to store for up to 3 months.

* To cook corn, husk ears, remove silk and rinse well. Place ears of corn in a large pot of boiling water and after returning to a boil, cook for 3 minutes. Cool ears in cold water. Cut kernels from cobs but do not scrape cobs.

Serving suggestions: Serve cold as a side dish, on an appetizer tray or as a topping on grilled fish, chicken or other meat entrées.

MAKES
5 CUPS

WATERMELON PICKLES

+ 1 (10 TO 12 LB.) SEEDLESS WATERMELON
+ 1 GAL. DISTILLED WATER, DIVIDED
+ 1 T. PICKLING SALT
+ 1 C. DISTILLED WHITE VINEGAR
+ 3½ C. SUGAR
+ 1½ TSP. WHOLE CLOVES
+ 2 CINNAMON STICKS
+ 2" CANDIED GINGER, OPTIONAL

DIRECTIONS

Cut watermelon slices 1" thick. Cut away the pink flesh (reserve for another use) and peel off the shiny outer skin from rind. Cut rind pieces into 1" chunks. Mix ½ gallon water and salt in a large bowl; add rind, cover and refrigerate overnight.

Drain and rinse rind with cold water. Soak rind in ice water for 2 hours and drain again. Boil remaining ½ gallon water and pour over rind in a large saucepan. Cook over medium heat until rind is fork tender but not soft, 10 to 15 minutes. Drain off water.

In another large pot, mix vinegar, sugar, cloves, cinnamon sticks and candied ginger. Bring syrup to a boil over medium heat, stirring frequently. Carefully add rind chunks to hot syrup and cook on low until rind is transparent, 20 to 25 minutes, stirring occasionally. Discard cloves, cinnamon sticks and ginger. Pack pickles into warm containers and cover with hot syrup. Cover tightly and let cool. Store containers in the refrigerator for up to 1 month.

TIP: COMBINE SPICES IN A SPICE BAG OR TEA INFUSER TO MAKE REMOVAL EASIER.

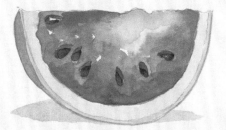

MAKES
1 QUART

Sliced Dill Pickles

- ✦ 2 TO 3 MEDIUM-SMALL CUCUMBERS
- ✦ 2 SPRIGS FRESH DILL
- ✦ 4½ TSP. PICKLING SALT
- ✦ 1 C. DISTILLED WHITE VINEGAR
- ✦ 1 C. DISTILLED WATER
- ✦ 1 SMALL CLOVE GARLIC, CRUSHED

DIRECTIONS

Cut off ends of each cucumber. Using a crinkle cutter, cut cucumbers into slices, ¼" thick. Measure out about 3 cups slices and set aside.

In a quart-size glass jar, combine dill, salt, vinegar, water and garlic; swirl jar to mix well. Add cucumber slices to fill jar but do not pack tightly. Leave about ½" headspace. Cover jar tightly and tip jar over once to mix cucumbers with brine. Place jar right side up in the refrigerator and let pickles soak for at least 24 hours before eating. Store pickles in the refrigerator for up to 1 month.

CUCUMBER TIP: LOOK FOR CUCUMBERS 3" TO 5" LONG FOR LARGE WHOLE DILLS OR PICKLE SLICES, CHUNKS OR SPEARS. "BURPLESS" SLICING CUCUMBERS ARE NOT THE BEST CHOICE FOR REFRIGERATED DILL PICKLES.

Index

Jams & Jellies

Pickles

& more

Preserving Summer's Bounty